ART FOR CHILDREN

MATISSE

PAINTER OF THE ESSENTIAL

By Yolande Baillet

Illustrated by Bernadette Theulet-Luzié

Translated by John Goodman

CHELSEA HOUSE PUBLISHERS

NEW YORK • PHILADELPHIA

I have a wonderful grandmother who has a great house with a terrific attic. Every year I spend a month there during summer vacation.

Grandma lives in Tourrette-sur-Loup. It's in the south of France, close to the Mediterranean coast. In Tourrette I have lots of friends to hang out with. We love adventure, and we like to explore the nearby moors. Fortunately for me, even in the month of August there are rainy days here, which are the kind I like best.

As soon as the first raindrop hits the pavement, I head up to the attic. I bound up the stairs four at a time and, my heart pacing, I open the attic door. Then I breathe in its beloved odor. After sneezing a few times, I begin my explorations, greeting some old friends along the way—after all, attics are full of ghosts.

In a corner of the room was a desk that I'd never thought to open before. But this year, for some strange reason, it attracted me. It was in very good condition—Grandma must have been keeping it polished. I opened the drawers and found some old papers and a few old books. There was also a pretty box covered in marbled paper whose colors had faded almost beyond recognition. It contained a thick packet of letters tied up in blue ribbon, some photographs of people I didn't recognize, and finally, a large notebook.

The notebook was a diary. Flipping through it quickly, I discovered that it was mostly about painting, especially that of Henri Matisse.

I knew that Matisse had lived in Nice and Vence, which were not far away. The diary interested me. I sat down, made myself as comfortable as possible, and started reading.

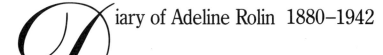

Diary of Adeline Rolin 1880–1942

April 1900

Today is my 20th birthday, today I arrive in Paris, today Edward, the man I love, is by my side. It's 1900, the beginning of a new century. For me, everything begins today—a day of brilliant sunlight!

May 1900

I'm exhausted from choosing curtains, carpets, and wallpaper. What color should the bedroom be? and the living room? and the study? What material should we use for the chairs? I was so obsessed by these questions that I ran all over Paris without seeing it at all. I was outside but thought only of interior decoration. Should it be Oriental, Baroque, or Louis XIV in style? Perhaps a bit of everything, with a Chinese screen, a small French settee, and small angels keeping watch over us.

Before reading any farther, I wanted to know a bit more about Adeline Rolin. Surely Grandma could tell me something about this notebook.

She smiled when she saw it in my hands. "Ah! Lisa, I see you've discovered Adeline's diary. She was my own grandmother, and this diary is a little treasure for anyone interested in painting."

September 1900

This morning I was at Ambroise Vollard's, the picture dealer. I love the atmosphere in his shop. And one meets artists there, painters and sculptors both. A thirty-year-old painter, wearing a bowler hat, oval glasses, and a black beard, spoke passionately about Cézanne. Vollard introduced us: Henri Matisse, Adeline Rolin. This Monsieur Matisse spoke to me about Cézanne with such enthusiasm that I bought one of the master's pictures.

December 1900

The year 1900 gets a grateful bow from me. I was applauding even before the footlights were out. While 1889 left us the Eiffel Tower, 1900 saw the opening of the Metro, the Paris subway system. The champagne flowed in torrents at Maxim's, and I cheered Sarah Bernhardt. Edward introduced me to everyone who's anyone in Paris, but I found the part of the city I like best in the bookshops, antique shops, and picture dealers.

Matisse about 1900.

March 1901

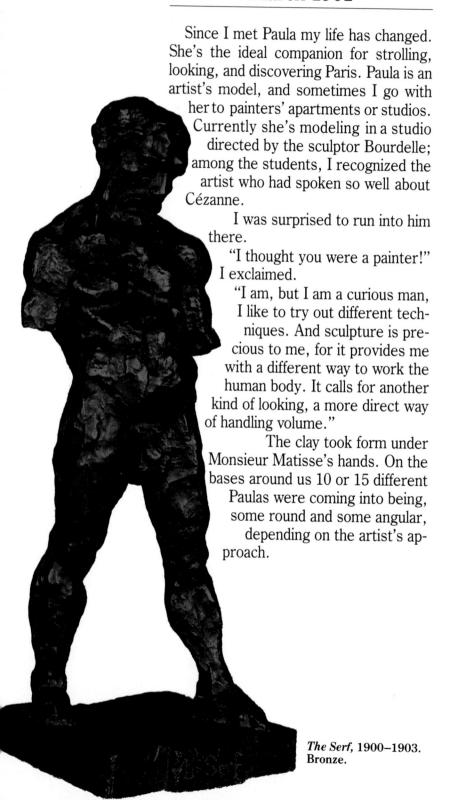

Since I met Paula my life has changed. She's the ideal companion for strolling, looking, and discovering Paris. Paula is an artist's model, and sometimes I go with her to painters' apartments or studios. Currently she's modeling in a studio directed by the sculptor Bourdelle; among the students, I recognized the artist who had spoken so well about Cézanne.

I was surprised to run into him there.

"I thought you were a painter!" I exclaimed.

"I am, but I am a curious man, I like to try out different techniques. And sculpture is precious to me, for it provides me with a different way to work the human body. It calls for another kind of looking, a more direct way of handling volume."

The clay took form under Monsieur Matisse's hands. On the bases around us 10 or 15 different Paulas were coming into being, some round and some angular, depending on the artist's approach.

The Serf, 1900–1903.
Bronze.

Artist's studios aren't the only places Paula takes me. We spend a lot of time at our favorite hat store. The milliner makes true masterpieces for us; some of her hats are decorated with young birds fighting each other in muslin nests. My most recent purchase is a marvelous little boater hat with a dove that is about to take flight and a garland of blue and white flowers serving as a ribbon.

I can just see them, Adeline and Paula, with their hats like wedding cakes, their rustling dresses, and their parasols.

"Did you know Adeline, Grandma?"
"Of course, and Paula, too! I went with them on their walks. We also passed in front of the art galleries to pay our respects to Picasso, Bonnard, and Matisse."
"You knew Picasso and Matisse?"
"Yes; they even pinched my cheeks!"
Goodness! My grandmother is famous and I didn't even know it!

I magine we're in northern France a hundred years ago, in a sad, gray town in Picardy called Cateau-Cambrésis. Matisse was born there on December 31, 1869. At the time, the local people farmed during spring and summer, while in the winter they supported themselves by weaving.

Shortly after Henri's birth, his father Emile, his brother Hippolyte, Henri, and his mother Héloise Gérard moved to Bohain, a small village close to Cateau. They ran a combination pharmacy and seed shop. Henri's future seemed clear: when he grew up he would take over his parents' business.

But chance decided otherwise. Henri's fragile health made it impractical for him to take over his father's shop, so in 1887, when he completed his high school studies at Saint-Quentin, he chose to pursue a legal career. For two years he studied law in Paris. He never visited a museum or an art exhibition until he was twenty years old, when the Universal

Henri Matisse in 1896.

Exposition of 1889 opened and the Eiffel Tower was built. Matisse became a law clerk in Saint-Quentin, but in 1890, an illness immobilized him. During his convalescence he tried painting for the first time, on the advice of a neighbor. To distract him, his mother gave him a box of paints and two cheap prints. Henri copied them and it was nothing short of a revelation for him—he decided then and there that he would study painting.

In order to do so, he returned to Paris. Matisse's father was not convinced that painting was his son's true calling but nonetheless paid for him to study at the School of Fine Arts in Paris under the serious and well-known master Bouguereau.

Matisse's studies were a disaster. The teaching was too rigidly academic, and Matisse felt he could not express himself. Matisse left the school, worked briefly at the less prestigious Julian Academy, and finally began to study with Gustave Moreau.

Matisse was happy with Moreau, later saying: "What a charming master he was. . . . I often went to the Louvre, but Moreau told us: 'Don't make do with going to museums, go into the street—that's where I learned to draw'."

In 1898 Matisse married Amélie Parayre, with whom he already had a daughter, named Marguerite.

After marrying, they traveled for a year, going from London to Ajaccio, Corsica, from fog to bright sunlight. Matisse adored the Mediterranean climate of Corsica. "I was dazzled there. Everything sparkles, everything is color and light," he said.

On returning home in 1899, he painted his *Orange Still Life*.

His son Jean was born the same year, and another son, Pierre, came into the world a year later, when Matisse started studying sculpture with Bourdelle. Matisse was having serious financial problems, so he and his family moved into his parents' home in Bohain. Relations between Henri and his father became strained, and the tense atmosphere made it difficult for Henri to work.

Orange Still Life, 1899.

January 1902

I barely had time to kiss his forehead— I leaned over him, and this beloved human being was gone. Such is the nature of time. It makes and then unmakes lives and seasons. How sad! Papa is no longer with us.

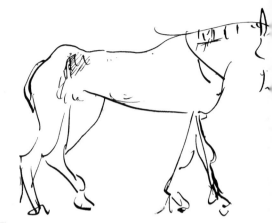

Drawing of a horse, 1900. Pen and ink on vellum paper, 6 inches × 9 inches.

May 1902

Yesterday Paula dragged me to the Champs-Elysées: "It will be good for you," she told me. The air was so sweet that we took a table at a sidewalk cafe. Was it chance, or is Paris as small as they say? I ran into Henri Matisse there.

"Some of my work is in a show at the Berthe Weill gallery," he told me. "That's why I'm in Paris. We're living at my parents' house in the country now."

August 1902

We spent a part of the summer at Deauville. Edward, who loves horses, was determined that I should share in his enthusiasm, but I'm not interested in riding. The smell of the stables turns my stomach, and I'd rather relax in a comfortable chair with a volume of poems by Stéphane Mallarmé.

February 1903

I went with Paula to visit one of her friends, a young Spanish painter named Pablo Picasso. He has dark hair and eyes and is very charming.

The Pont des Arts and the Louvre in Paris.

Studio under the Eaves,
1903.
**Oil on canvas, 1 foot 10
inches × 1 foot 6 inches.**

June 1904

Finally! Matisse is holding an exhibition at Vollard's gallery—his first all to himself.

This time our meeting wasn't a matter of chance, and Edward accompanied me. He likes painting, but his real passion is horse racing. Monsieur Matisse was delighted by this: "If I weren't a painter, I'd have loved to be a jockey or a musician," he told us.

October 1904

I saw the Autumn Salon, the artistic event of the season. This year it featured a large Cézanne exhibition. It seemed likely that I would run into Matisse there, but there was a surprise for me—he, too, had work on show. He led us to his 12 canvases. As Paula said, "This is an artist to follow!" There are times when it seems like one can't take two steps in Paris without meeting the same person, and this year it was almost as though Matisse and I were the only people in the city. I'm exaggerating, of course. There was also the milliner, Paula, Edward, and our coachman—at least until Edward decides to buy an automobile.

May 1905

"In May, do what you like," they say. What I like this season, what really suits me, are dresses by Paul Poiret. This spring I'll wear nothing but white. I'll still have a delicate waist, but I won't wear corsets anymore—*that* hell is over for me.

Paula and I went to the Boulogne park, and we were in the mood to confide in one another. Paula said she's in love with a lieutenant. Matisse, who is very practical, would say that "a model in love is a bad model," because "they want Saturdays off, and Sundays—and then what happens to my work?" But Paula isn't modeling for Matisse.

"Tell me, grandma, did Adeline model, too?"

"I think she mostly watched, but sometimes she picked up some charcoal and drew Paula or made quick sketches of the painter at work."

"Quick sketches?"

"Yes. You know drawings that capture a pose in a few quick strokes."

"Do painters make quick sketches, too?"

"Of course, lots of them. As soon as they think of a painting, they make quick drawings and sketches. In the street they sketch passersby, workers, whoever, just the way others would take snapshots."

Luxe, Calme et Volupté 1904. Oil on canvas, 2 feet 10 inches × 3 feet 10 inches.

"Scandalous! Scandalous! By God, such colors! Who are these young people who call themselves painters and scribble such pathetic canvases?"—these were the responses evoked by a certain room in the Autumn Salon. I know all the artists in question, beginning with Matisse, who is showing three portraits. There are also works by André Derain, Othon Friesz, Georges Rouault, and Maurice de Vlaminck. One journalist called them *fauves* or "wild beasts." Certainly their works are unusual, but it's about time something other than stale, conventional painting was exhibited.

"What was so strange about these canvases?"

"Hmm. . . . Wait, I think that . . ."

Grandma pulled a book from her shelves. "Here we are! *The Green Line (Portrait of Madame Matisse)*, 1905. This is one of the paintings Adeline would have seen at the Autumn Salon. In this painting Matisse used very bright colors, pure ones applied to the canvas just as they came out of the tube. The Autumn Salon was an official exhibition open to the public. You can imagine how shocked some of the visitors were. They weren't prepared for what they saw."

"Was Matisse the first to paint like this?"

"No. He has his own style, of course, but the same saturated colors were used by Gauguin."

Grandma showed me *The Yellow Christ* by Gauguin.

The Green Line (Portrait of Madame Matisse), 1905. Oil on canvas, 1 foot 4 inches × 1 foot 1 inch.

May 1906

Paula's amorous adventure came to an end. The lieutenant was transferred with his garrison, and there was no question of Paula's leaving Paris, except to go on a short vacation or to work with a painter. But artists rarely take their models with them when they travel. Speaking of artists on the move, I've just learned that Matisse is in Algiers, in North Africa.

Nijinsky in *Scheherazade* in 1910. Ballet by Fokine, costume by Leon Bakst.

Nijinsky and Karsavina in *Le Spectre de la Rose*, ballet by Fokine, produced in 1911 by Diaghilev's Ballets Russes.

I may be very pregnant, but I wasn't about to miss the inauguration of Matisse's school. Is that unreasonable? That's what Edward said, begging for me to stay in bed. Paula said it too, and she promised to tell me all the latest gossip she heard there. But I decided that nothing was going to make me miss this important occasion.

The idea for the school was not Matisse's, but was first proposed by his admirers Leo, Sarah, Gertrude, and Michael Stein. What a project for Matisse, who had such a hard time finding a good teacher! Would he be the ideal master?

"Was he a good teacher, grandma?"

"Yes, but he didn't teach for long. Matisse wanted each of his students to find their own way and to develop their own sensibility, but the ones who came to him wanted to paint and draw just like him. That wasn't what he wanted, and the school took up too much of his time. He had to choose between painting and teaching."

"And Adeline?"

"She had a little boy, my father, Franklin."

March 1909

Yesterday I went to see Matisse in his studio in Issy-le-Moulineaux. He's working on a mural commissioned by the Russian collector Shchukin. On the paper pinned to the wall, the dancers moved in a circle. Matisse hummed as he drew.

"You're in a very good mood today, Monsieur Matisse."

"I'm humming for my dancers" he answered me, smiling. "It's a dance tune from the south of France I heard at the Moulin de la Galette."

I thought he was going to ask me to dance, but he didn't. Paula would have said, "How odd this Monsieur Matisse is!"

June 1910

Marvelous! Fantastic! Stravinsky's *Firebird* took us far away, to a world of magic and fairytales. The Ballets Russes and its director Serge Diaghilev are taking the art of dance to unforeseen heights. Paula, who dreams of being a dancer, couldn't stop ogling Michel Fokine, the choreographer.

The Dance, 1910. Oil on canvas, 8 feet 6 inches × 12 feet 10 inches.

View from the Window,
1912. Oil on canvas, 2
feet 6 inches x 4 feet 3
inches.

December 1911

Matisse is a real nomad—it's as though distance means nothing to him. He sent me a postcard from Seville. A few days later I heard he was in Issy. By the time I got out to his studio he had gone to

Collioure and had tickets to Moscow in his pocket. "And then," he said to me, "I'm going to Tangier until the spring comes. Luckily, it only takes an easel to transform a hotel room into a studio."

June 1912

I think trips renew our energies and make it easier for us to face the challenges ahead. I'm in Tangier, and I'm dazzled by the blue here, which turns from turquoise to ultramarine as the sky merges with the sea. I already experienced this sensation in front of a canvas Matisse painted here last year. I was in the studio in Issy-les-Moulineaux, and I couldn't pull myself away from his *View from a Window*. There wasn't a hint of wind, and heat seemed to fall over me. I surrendered to the feeling of calm and balance that radiated from the picture.

Tangier, Morocco, early in the 20th century.

May 1913

The big event this month was the ballet *The Rite of Spring*—first, because it marked the opening of the new Champs-Elysées Theater, and second, because new Ballets Russes productions are always an event. But poor Stravinsky, who had to flee before the insults hurled at him by the furious audience; and poor Nijinsky, whose choreography was brilliant but completely misunderstood; and poor Serge Diaghilev, who had sunk so much money and energy into this venture. And poor us—our frantic applause didn't have a chance against the booing and hissing of the rest of the crowd.

September 1914

War took us by surprise. We stared at the ocean and remained light-hearted at first, but today I walk through Deauville in a nurse's uniform.

Every day brings new horrors. Fortunately, Paula writes to me and keeps me informed about the art world and its reaction to the war. The enlisted now include Blaise Cendrars, Guillaume Apollinaire, and André Derain. Those not serving for one reason or another try to create in the midst of anguish and disorder: Matisse, Picasso, Juan Gris . . .

Right: *Interior with Goldfish,* **1914. Oil on canvas, 4 feet 10 inches × 3 feet 2 inches.**

Below: French foot soldiers during an attack in 1914.

December 1914, Collioure

Dear Madame,

I learned from your charming friend, Paula Lecuyer, that the war has both made you a nurse and troubled your heart.

We don't know how long this war will last, but we must continue to create. For us, as artists, it is the only way we can participate.

I'm sorry I can't show you the paintings that I made this spring in Issy. They have the colors you love, and their subjects — open windows, studio views, and goldfish — would lighten your heart.

In Collioure I ran into Juan Gris, who is, as you know, a Cubist painter. We had some long conversations — it is comforting to talk about art in these difficult times. As the light is quite beautiful now, I will return to my work. But I hope to see you soon.

Fondly,

Henri Matisse

April 1916

Soon it will be two years since war broke out. My new life has fallen into place—sometimes I'm a nurse, sometimes I'm a mother, and I never have enough time! When I go to Vollard's gallery, I look at the paintings as if they were mirages; nothing seems less real than a Renoir or a Monet. Sometimes I go to see Matisse in Paris or in Issy-les-Moulineaux. There's a lot of black in his canvases and also a new way of composing, of handling space. Could this be due to Cubist influence?

The Piano Lesson, 1916. Oil on canvas, 8 feet × 7 feet.

Juan Gris, *Still Life with Book*, 1913. Oil on canvas, 1 foot 6 inches × 1 foot.

The term *cubism* obviously comes from the word *cube*, but I still didn't know what it meant. Grandma, who knows a lot about art, came to my aid.

"Remember that in 1914 Matisse had conversations with Juan Gris, the Cubist painter. It shouldn't surprise us that their exchanges influenced their work. The Cubists began with the idea that everything in nature can be represented in geometric shapes. Matisse didn't go as far as they did, but he adopted some Cubist procedures that suited him. Look at this painting, *The Piano Lesson*. Matisse gives us a few elements familiar to us: a window, a seated woman, the face of a little boy, a sculpture. The setting is clearly a room, but we don't see either the floor or the walls. Everything is against the same gray ground, and the space is crossed by straight and oblique lines. Here Matisse cast space in geometrical forms, like the Cubists did with nature.

Right: *Portrait of Greta Prozor*, Paris 1916. Oil on canvas, 4 feet 9 inches × 3 feet 2 inches.

Below: In Auguste Renoir's studio in Cagnes-sur-Mer, 1917. Seated, from left: the actress Greta Prozor, Auguste Renoir. Standing, from left: Claude Renoir, Henri Matisse, Pierre Renoir.

Dear Adeline,

I've been at the coast barely two days, and I haven't had a second to myself. I spent the day yesterday in Cagnes, at Auguste Renoir's house. What a wonderful man, and what a terrific artist—who paints women better than he?

Ah, don't tell me you think Matisse does. In fact, he just came to see Renoir. Auguste was very hard on him; the two of them certainly paint very differently.

Renoir, is such a sensual painter. Skin is like velvet to him, tempting him to caress it. He told Matisse straight out that he considered him a bad painter. "But," he said, "when you use black, which is a difficult color, you do so with such perfect judgement that you must be a good painter." Today I'm resting. Tomorrow I return to Cagnes, where we'll have tea and cake, and where the odor of rabbit being cooked with herbs will tickle my nose while I pose. I'm looking forward to seeing you soon.

Love,

Paula

The Café de la Paix in Paris, 1921.

Sweet Adeline,

What a pity you couldn't accompany me on this trip. I learned a great deal at the medical congress about new discoveries and research projects. But fortunately there were friends here to distract me, and yesterday—you will have guessed this part already—I went to see Henri Matisse.

He is currently preparing sets and costumes for Diaghilev's ballet *The Song of the Nightingale,* which is to have music by Stravinsky. You know how much Henri loves music and dance, and you can imagine how wrapped up he is in this project. He's going to London with the ballet troupe.

Before leaving him, I made him promise to come and see us in Paris. He'll be in the city soon, for he's about to exhibit some recent work at the Bernheim-Jeune gallery.

I can't wait to get home; give Frankie a hug for me. I love you with all my heart.

Edward

November 1918

Finally, the armistice has been signed! God grant that peace and happiness will return to us.

May 1920

Today is my 40th birthday, and yet I've never felt younger or more free.

We go out every night to an exhibition opening, the ballet, or the theater. Paris is more than ever the cultural capital of the Old World.

Edward bought a Citroën automobile, Paula wears her hair in a bob, and our skirts are so short that they reveal our ankles and calves.

Paula and I have sworn allegiance to a single fashion designer — Gabrielle Chanel.

When Edward is away on business, Paula teaches me to dance the tango. We're as crazy now as we were in our twenties!

The Citroën Torpedo in 1920.

édo 4 places "Série".

Henri Matisse drew and painted many odalisques, or images of reclining women in Oriental garb. At work in 1928.

I'm in Nice for a few weeks. This morning I went to the flower market, and then to see Matisse on the Place Charles Félix. I was greeted by the powerful perfume of giant anemones—Henri's favorite flower. He always has flowers—lots of flowers—around him in vases or old bottles, but also on wallpaper, upholstery, rugs, and curtains. His model Henriette was there, dressed as an odalisque and lounging on a sofa.

More than ever, Henri's studio seemed like a theater. A theater for which he was the set designer, the make-up artist, the costume designer, the director, and finally, even the audience.

I arrived in the middle of a modeling session. I didn't want to disturb him, so I made myself as inconspicuous as possible and watched. I observed the painter and his model. Henri was very close to Henriette; sometimes he spoke with her, sometimes he looked at her with a disturbing intensity.

Henri took his charcoal and drew, making the same drawing 10, 20, 30 times! Finally, exhausted by making all these studies, he took up a brush and traced a simple line drawing with such ease that it seemed he'd memorized her face, her body, and all the flowers around her. Henri is in love with the curved line, the arabesque. Angles are rare and lines are flexible in his work; forms seem to blossom under his hand.

I took my time walking home. I felt like my head was empty, for what I'd seen had upset me.

"Is it really that unnerving to see a painter work, grandma?"

"First of all, to see Matisse work, even once, was a special privilege, because he required absolute quiet to concentrate and to create. And then his connection with his models was so intense that it was troubling, for he drew with and through passionate love."

Odalisque in Turkish Pants, **1920–1921. Pen and black ink with pencil and white ink retouches on vellum paper, 11 inches × 1 foot 3 inches.**

Inside the image:
26 - EXPOSITION INTERNATIONALE
DES ARTS DÉCORATIFS — PARIS - 1925
PÉNICHES PAUL POIRET
« AMOURS » pour la présentation des Créations de la Maison Martine
«DÉLICES» pour la présentation des Créations de la Maison Rosine (avec annexion d'un restaurant)
« ORGUES » pour la présentation des Élégances de la Maison PAUL POIRET   A. P.
(avec annexion d'orgues lumineuses - Création spéciale)
Thé dansant
Soupers dansants
EDITIONS M FORTIER

Postcard from the International Decorative Arts Exposition of 1925.

April 1924

When you spend a lot of time going to fancy costume balls, the seriousness that prevails in some painters' work can seem surprising, to say the least.

Yesterday we went to the opening of an exhibition of paintings by Georges Rouault. His work is full of anguish and depicts the world as corrupt. Had we party creatures been invited to this sad gathering to make a point?

December 1925

This year has been so rich in events of all sorts that I haven't had time to write a single line.

In April, there was the Exposition of the Decorative Arts. The art deco style was all the fashion there and was used on everything from furniture to jewelry to table sculpture.

In August, Charlie Chaplin's movie *The Gold Rush* opened, creating a sensation.

In October, Paula and I went to see the fall fashion collections. Hemlines are above the knee, waists are low, and profiles are dominated by straight lines. That evening we went to the Champs-Elysées Theater to see *La Revue Nègre*. The stars, Josephine Baker and Sidney Bechet, were extraordinary.

Finally in November, we went to see a Surrealist exhibition. Andre Breton, the group's founder, was represented, as were Max Ernst, Juan Miró, Pablo Picasso, Giorgio de Chirico, Hans Arp, and Man Ray.

To finish up the year in style, Edward is taking me to Italy—to Venice, Florence, and Rome. Perhaps we'll run into Henri there, who's renewing his creative juices by looking at Giotto's frescoes in Padua, not far from Venice.

Josephine Baker.

Sidney Bechet.

Paula was in high form when she arrived at my apartment this afternoon. She was wearing a flattering pink dress and a little felt hat. She could speak of nothing but the Tuileries Salon exhibition.

"Well, my dear Adeline, there was only one canvas I really liked, and—you're not going to believe this—it was by Henri Matisse! That man certainly is full of surprises. All the critics are saying the same thing: he's an artist who's always growing and who never stops looking for new color combinations and types of compositions. I cut out some of the reviews in the papers this morning. Just listen:

It is anything but displeasing to see a painter who is in absolute control of his craft and who has long since accustomed us to his perfectly harmonious compositions strike out in a new direction. For my part, I consider this fearlessness an advantage, and I love this work's deliberately deformed figure, which has all the charm of a sketch, and its wildly varied color scheme, which reveals an unrivaled eye. There isn't another artist alive who's capable of using color to achieve an effect that's simultaneously so intense and so harmonious.

Georges Charensol

On the other hand, there are a few paintings that do honor to the Tuileries Salon, including a Matisse that is moving in its freshness and is a canvas that convinces one of the power of art. It is without doubt the most striking and attractive work in the Salon. After looking at this painting, one no longer fears old age, because it proves that the mind can remain eternally young. The colors are remarkably rich. . . . Astonishing!

E. Teriade

Decorative Figure Against an Ornamental Ground. Nice, 1925–26. Oil on canvas, 4 feet 3 inches × 3 feet 3 inches.

"The canvas is called *Decorative Figure against an Ornamental Ground.* Everything else pales by comparison. To be fair, in some respects this Matisse resembles a work by Chagall, and a good one."

"If Paula has come to like Matisse, what are we coming to?" Edward joked. But Paula, who was still heady from the experience, didn't hear him, and the whirlwind of pink muslin disappeared.

May 21, 1927

The Place de l'Opéra was jammed with people, and the boulevards were mobbed. We all wanted to see Charles Lindbergh, but no such luck; Frank, his wife, and I, lost in the crowd, missed him. His Atlantic crossing is a marvelous achievement. Will mechanical birds soon be transporting us above the clouds and over oceans with the speed of the wind? What a strange thought!

January 28, 1929

This morning, Frank came to announce the birth of their little girl: Alice Emile Rolin.

June 1930

Dear friend,

I promised you a report from the islands, so here it is. Lounging, walking, fishing, and eating are my sole activities. Everything here is beautiful, too beautiful, so beautiful that one feels crushed. It has disabled me. I won't touch a single brush. You know how I've always been taken with light and its poetry. I wanted to see what it was like below the equator. It is gold, while ours is silver.

On my way here, I made a stop in New York. The city electrified me and made me feel full of energy. The light in New York is exceptionally beautiful, and there are those towers, those masses rising into the air in the crystalline light. I asked myself: Why go so far? But I'll tell you more about that later. I'm taking a few photographs and doing a little sketching. But the most important of what I've seen I'm keeping to myself: I want to let my impressions ripen.

Warm regards to Edward. See you soon.

Henri Matisse

May 1930

To each his own Atlantic crossing—Henri has left to conquer the Pacific Islands and the New World, not by air, but by boat, like a pirate. I'm waiting to hear from him.

Left: Lindbergh in front of his plane (top photo) and in Paris with Painlevé, the French war minister, and Blériot, another great aviator (bottom).

Window in Tahiti. Nice, 1935–1936. Oil on canvas, 9 inches x 7 inches.

May 1931

I arranged to visit Henri this morning. I knew he was very busy (he's working on a wall decoration commissioned during his trip to the United States by Dr. Barnes), so I certainly wasn't expecting an airplane flight.

That sounds crazy. Let me explain. When I entered his new studio, he took me by the arm:

"Come, dear friend, prepare to fly, for I'm going to show you *The Dance*."

Just imagine hovering over this composition, like an aviator getting his first view of the earth's extent. It was a dizzying experience!

"With my *Dance* decoration I wanted to create a sensation of flight, of freedom, as though the dancers were merging with the architecture rather than being restricted by it, so that the effect of harmony, of fusion between painting and architecture, was complete," Henri told me.

For work on *The Dance,* Henri had rented an old movie studio in Nice. He did not make any preliminary sketches, but instead worked on it at full scale and in the final format. It was large, and he had to use a bit of charcoal attached to a long piece of bamboo to draw it. When the time came to add color, he used large pieces of painted paper which he cut and assembled like the pieces of a puzzle.

The Dance (first version), 1931–32. Watercolor, 1 foot × 2 feet 8 inches.

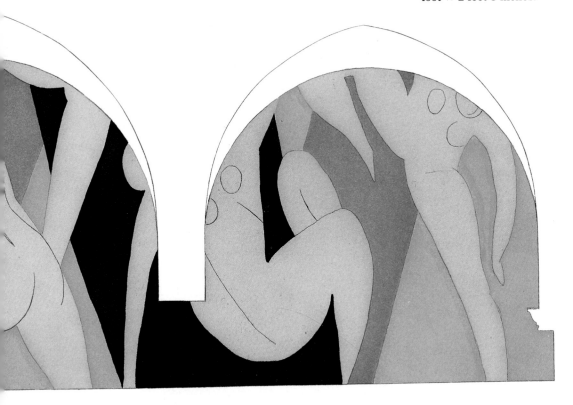

February 1932

"What do you think of these reliefs, Adeline?" Edward asked me.

"They're interesting," I answered.

"Interesting!" Edward exclaimed. "Why they're marvelous, colossal! What superb work, dear Henri! For once, don't pay any attention to my wife—while she has an eye for painting, she understands nothing of sculpture. Believe me, these four *Backs* provide a graceful illustration of how you work. The treatment of volume in the fourth version is absolutely remarkable. If I were rich, I wouldn't hesitate to say: I'll take it!"

Rash Edward! If we were rich, we wouldn't have enough room in our house by now for even a flea.

The Back III, 1916–17. Bronze, 6 feet 3 inches × 3 feet 9 inches × 6 inches.

The Back IV, 1930.
Bronze, 6 feet 3 inches
× 3 feet 9 inches × 6
inches.

April 1933

This afternoon, Henri showed me some lithographs he'd made between 1920 and 1925. They took my breath away. Admittedly, I've long admired his work, but seeing these odalisques gave me immense pleasure. Here this great colorist had used all his considerable intelligence to capture the rustle of fine fabrics and the ease of his models using only white, gray, and dark black.

His elegant line defines the arabesques, flowers, and objects, as well as the model. Henri sees every object, fabric, or model as a piece of love—in his art, nothing happens by chance, everything is the product of reflection and emotion.

These lithographs also reveal the man who haunted the halls of the Louvre and copied works by the great masters hanging on its walls. Matisse knows that no one lives or creates in isolation, and that the influence of others is not something to avoid, for it nourishes the artist's imagination.

November 1934

I'd love it if I could avoid thinking about politics and current events, but in these difficult times they demand attention. In Germany, Adolf Hitler's party is spreading racist and anti-Semitic ideas. In Italy, Mussolini rules as a dictator and tramples on individual liberties. In Paris, political demonstrations are not uncommon, and sometimes they result in violent confrontations between the supporters of opposing parties.

Everywhere in the world, political instability prevails. I fear the worst, so I applauded enthusiastically after Jean Cocteau's play *The Infernal Machine* at the Champs-Elysées Theater. I was expressing my love of freedom of expression more than my liking for the play itself. What would we do if a dictator made us be silent? What would then be the fate of art and the human imagination?

The Dream, 1935. Oil on canvas, 2 feet 7 inches × 2 feet 2 inches.

October 1935

What to think? What to say? Once again, I'm in love with one of Henri's paintings: *The Dream*. Lydia Delectorskaya, who posed for this canvas, brought out something fresh and natural in the artist. One can feel the canvas breathing underneath the image, and the forms have been reduced to their essentials.

"Ah!" Grandma interrupted. "Lydia Delectorskaya was to become an important figure in Matisse's work. She became not only his model but also his assistant and his secretary. She remained with him until the end of his life."

Pierre Bonnard, *Late Afternoon Nap, or In a Southern Garden*. Oil on canvas.

May 1936

This was an afternoon of laughter and tears. Paula and I dug out some old photographs and souvenirs.

Here was Apollinaire, who so charmed Paula when we went to La Rotonde one night.

And Picasso, who so loved theatricals, and Cendrars, who told us all about his dangerous travels, and so many others who passed through our lives! Pierre Bonnard and Edouard Vuillard, both romantics at heart; the quiet Andre Rouveure; Henri, back when I was still calling him Monsieur Matisse; Albert Marquet; and André Derain.

Today, all the artists Paula thought were worth following are regarded as the greatest of our time.

Happily, the moment to take a final reckoning has not yet arrived, and although Paula and I are already 56 years old, and Henri 67, we still feel young. We keep track of new artists and movements with just as much enthusiasm as before.

July 1937

The Universal Exposition is open, and we couldn't wait to go. We've watched the pavilions rising and the gradual transformation of the site into a fairground.

The Eiffel Tower looks down on it with an arrogant air. The German and Russian pavilions are exactly opposite one another, and seem ready for battle. But what Paula and I most wanted to see was Picasso's painting *Guernica*, in the Spanish pavilion.

1938

Henri is moving to the heights above Nice, to the old Regina Hotel in Cimiez. It's a superb building suggestive of a time when the Russian Czars gave sumptuous parties every night. Henri is drawing a great deal, and the images from Tahiti are finally seeing the light of day. I've seen several linoleum prints—strange portraits that seem like negatives, with white lines standing out prominently against a black ground. Henri's mastery of contrast and line has never been more evident. In these works he's moving toward even greater simplicity and reduction of form. Truly, he is the painter of the essential.

The Universal Exposition of 1937.

Above: View from the Eiffel Tower toward the Palais de Chaillot.

Below: The Palais de Chaillot and the Iena Bridge, with the facing Soviet and German pavilions.

January 28, 1939

Today is Alice's tenth birthday. Pau[l] gave her a record of Charles Trenet sing[g]ing "The Sun has a Rendez-vous with th[e] Moon." Watching those two laugh an[d] dance, I couldn't help but ask myse[lf] which of them was the crazier.

March 1939

Dance is still, and will always be, th[e] motor of Henri's work. Léonide Massin[e] the choreographer of the Ballets Russe[s] has commissioned him to do the sets f[or] his new piece, *Red and Black*. The Ba[l]lets Russes have again turned to a famou[s] painter.

The Beautiful Tahitian Woman, 1938. Linoleum print, 11 inches × 8 inches.

September 3, 1939

Human madness has once again overtaken us—war has broken out! Times of pain and suffering have returned.

The Loves, illustration of
a poem by Pierre de
Ronsard. Lithograph,
1938.

November 1941

I could well sum up my day with the phrase "at a sick man's bedside." But this was no ordinary sick man!

Early this year Henri had a serious operation. Yesterday I went to see the Risen One, as the nurses had nicknamed him, and he's a rock! A solid block of pure willpower!

What do you think he talked to me about?

"Work, dear Adeline, is the only thing that can save me from pain and boredom. I'm bedridden, of course, but with Ronsard's poems to keep me company there's never a dull moment. Reading his songs and sonnets, I see the faces and flowers I will use to illustrate them. I feel lightheaded, almost like a young man or an eternal lover!"

The diary stops there, suddenly, in 1941. I looked up to find in my grandmother's eyes an answer to the sad question I didn't dare ask.

She looked down and murmured "January 2, 1942, from pneumonia."

In the course of a few hours I had met my great-great grandmother and a great painter. I had lost Adeline, whose diary was in my lap, and this made me sad.

But I wanted to know the end of Matisse's story. What became of the eternal lover?

"Come," my grandmother said. "Let's not think about all that any more. Let's pick some raspberries, and we'll make a pudding this afternoon."

Outside, the rain had stopped. As soon as we entered the garden the fragrances of the damp earth washed over us. The raspberry, rose, and lupine bushes made soft rustling noises.

"This is the best moment to pick this fruit," Grandma said. "Tomorrow it will be spoiled."

But I wasn't listening; I was thinking about the diary.

"Grandmother, why don't we finish Adeline's diary ourselves?"

Grandma is as terrific as her house and as nifty as her attic, so she said yes right away.

The pudding was delicious, and the night was beautiful.

Grandma promised me that tomorrow we'll go to Nice. And Nice rhymes with Matisse!

It was almost noon when we reached Salea Square, with its flower market. There were lots of pinks and bougainvillaeas. Farther along, the merchants had their stalls all year around. We bought some mushrooms preserved in oil, some olives, and some almonds. The last shops we visited were on the Place Charles Félix. I closed my eyes in hopes of smelling turpentine or hearing the rustle of charcoal being drawn over paper. But the hawkers' voices brought me back to reality. There wasn't even a plaque to indicate that Matisse had lived here 60 years ago!

atisse in 1947.

We followed the English Walk for a moment, looking at the sea as Matisse must have done quite often.

Finally, we arrived at the Matisse Museum. It's in a lovely villa dating from the 17th century. While grandma had some tea in the museum cafeteria, I started my tour.

My heart pacing, I entered the first room. Penetrating Matisse's universe felt like visiting a friend, and I discovered what great pleasure and emotion one can derive from painting. Just like in Adeline's diary, I could follow the painter here step by step. I immediately recognized a portrait of Madame Matisse from the fauve period, entitled *Head of Lorette*, that conveyed the model's personality to a tee, and then my gaze fell on an *Odalisque with a Red Chest*.

"That must be Henriette!"

And then I saw *The Dance*, not the final version, which is in the Barnes Collection outside Philadelphia, but a preparatory version made out of cut paper.

"Here," a loud voice said behind me, "Matisse used paper cuttings to try out different color schemes, to find the perfect balance. Later, he would use this technique to make large-scale compositions and a remarkably illustrated book called *Jazz*."

The loud voice belonged to a man with a moustache who was accompanied by his young son.

Head of Lorette, Green Background. Paris, 1916. Oil on canvas, 1 foot 2 inches × 11 inches.

The cut-paper compositions were in another room. Seeing them, I thought about Adeline.

In her diary she had written that Matisse was "the painter of the essential." What she meant by that remark became clear as I looked at *The Creole Dancer, The Blue Nude,* and *The Sea. The Creole Dancer* is a colorful work in which the dancer is suggested by the simple shapes of an oval and a triangle. Her limbs take the form of curved lines that recall a dancer's movements.

"With this cut-paper technique Matisse achieved a radical simplification of form, retaining only those elements necessary to evoke the represented object."

The Horse, the Equerry, and the Clown, 1943–44. Painted cut paper glued to canvas.

Blue Nude II, 1952. Cut paper, 3 feet 10 inches × 2 feet 11 inches.

The loud voice was behind me again, and the little boy's eyes were wide open. I don't think he'd understood any of it!

But I wasn't done with these cut-paper compositions just yet. On the second floor, the book *Jazz* awaited me. *Jazz* consists of twenty bright watercolors. Each one appears opposite a short text that Matisse wrote with his painter's brush. Several of the illustrations evoke the circus: *The Sword-Swallower, Monsieur Loyal, The Clown.* What would Adeline have thought of them? My own favorite was *Pierrot's Burial.*

I found Grandma in front of *The Bees*.

—"Ah, there you are! Look, this is a design for the chapel in Vence. At the end of his life Matisse took on a major project, the decoration of the Dominican Chapel of the Rosary in Vence. It was to be the crowning achievement of his career."

We went down to the bookshop. Grandmother bought me a book on Matisse with lots of reproductions. We talked about his paintings, *Jazz*, and the chapel.

We had to wait until the next day to visit the chapel. Before going inside, I closed my eyes tight and tried to summon the presence of Adeline. When I opened my eyes again, they beheld a marvelous sight; like magic, thousands of tiny spots of colored light were strewn over the floor and sparkled on the walls.

Matisse had said: "When I enter the chapel, I feel that my whole being is present in it." In the same way, I felt Adeline's presence in these brilliant colors.

In front of us, a guide was giving a tour.

"The chapel is effectively divided into two. On one side are the colored windows, while on the other everything is in black and white ceramic."

Bronze crucifix for the Chapel of the Rosary in Vence.

Pale Blue Window (design for the apse window in the Chapel of the Rosary in Vence). Left: detail. Right: the entire composition. Painted and cut paper glued to kraft paper, then fixed to white paper on canvas, 16 feet 11 inches × 8 feet 3 inches.

Matisse working on the Vence chapel in 1950–51.

"It's a little like *Jazz*," grandmother observed. "there's a dialogue between color on one hand and black and white on the other."

"For his *Tree of Life* window," the guide continued, "Matisse chose three colors: ultramarine blue, lemon yellow, and bottle green. The ceramic tiles are decorated with line drawings. Matisse wanted the final effect to be pure and light."

I again recalled Adeline's remark about Matisse and the essential.

Next the guide showed us the priests' robes, which were decorated with white designs that looked like paper cuttings.

The tour was coming to an end. The guide didn't know it, but he was closing Adeline's diary again.

"Having finished the chapel, Matisse had lots of other plans: 'I'm only 83 years old,' he said. Two years later, on November 3, 1954, in Nice, Henri Matisse died, making it necessary for us to imagine the future of art without him."

A Painting's Evolution

Successive versions of *The Rumanian Blouse*. Above: third and fifth versions. Above right: eighth version.

Each work of art has its history, and *The Rumanian Blouse* is a case in point.

Matisse loved to look for unusual objects in junk-shops.

"I found a beautiful old Rumanian blouse with faded red stitching that must have belonged to a princess." He was fascinated by the designs on this blouse, and in 1937, he started to draw it.

In November of 1939, he started a painting of it that would not be completed until nine months later. Matisse had photographs made, recording each stage of his work on it. In all, there are 13 of these photographs.

"I have an idea in my head and I set out to realize it. Quite often I find myself recasting it as I work. . . . But I know where I'm going. The photographs make it possible for me determine whether the last version is closer to my original idea than the earlier versions, whether I'm advancing or going backwards."

Looking at these photographs today, what do we see?

A young woman wearing a Rumanian blouse comes closer and closer, looking right at us. She soon takes up the entire field of the painting, making it easier for us to admire her blouse. Each successive rendering of it makes it seem more puffed up. The decorations in the background gradually disappear, as does her chair, allowing the patterns on the blouse to stand out against a monochrome red background.

The Rumanian Blouse and the 13 photographs were exhibited for the first time in 1945. At the opening of the show at the Maeght Gallery, a critic exclaimed: "So there's all this behind a Matisse!"

Above: eleventh and twelfth versions.
Left: *The Rumanian Blouse,* 1940. Oil on canvas, 3 feet × 2 feet 5 inches.

GLOSSARY

anemone: a member of the buttercup family with brightly colored flowers

anti-Semitism: hostility toward or discrimination against Jews as a religious or racial group

apse: a projecting part of a building that is usually vaulted

arabesque: a complicated pattern of intertwined lines

armistice: a truce

art deco: a popular decorative style of the 1920s and 1930s marked by bold outlines, streamlined forms, and the use of new materials such as plastic

aviator: the pilot of a plane

boater: a stiff straw hat

charcoal: a pencil used in drawing that is black and is easily blended

choreographer: one who arranges or directs the movement in a dance

composition: the arrangement of forms in a work of art

corset: a women's close-fitting boned undergarment that extends from the bust or waist to below the hips

cubism: a style of abstract art that shows sever views of the same object at once and breaks object down to their basic geometrical shapes

fauvism: a style of art characterized by vivid color free treatment of form, and a decorative effect; th word *fauvism* comes from the French word *fauve* which means wild beast

Impressionism: a school of painting that used dab or strokes of unmixed color to simulate actual reflecte light

kraft paper: a strong paperboard

linoleum: a material made from a linseed-oil-base resin and a cloth backing that is used for making prints

lithograph: a print made from a flat plate

milliner: a person who makes hats

The Matisse Museum in Nice, France.

Matisse in 1953.

monochrome: of one color

moor: a boggy area not used for farming or other purposes

mural: a work of art such as a painting that is applied to and made part of a wall or ceiling

oblique: a line that is neither perpendicular nor parallel

odalisque: a female figure in the dress of a concubine in a harem

surrealism: a school of painting marked by fantastic imagery or unnatural combinations

vellum: a strong, cream-colored paper

Chronology

1869: Henri Matisse is born December 31, in Cateau-Cambrésis, France.

1887–1888: Goes to Paris to study law.

1889: Becomes a law clerk in Saint-Quentin; studies drawing at the Ecole Quentin-Latour.

1890: Paints his first canvases.

1892: Settles in Paris, takes courses in art first from Bouguereau, then from Gabriel Ferrier; enters contest for admission to the Ecole des Beaux-Arts, but fails to qualify.

1895: Gustave Moreau takes him into his studio at the Beaux-Arts; Matisse takes a trip to Brittany.

1896: Makes his first submission to the Salon of the Société Nationale des Beaux-Arts; vacations at Belle-Isle.

1898: Marries Amelie Alexandrine Parayre on January 8; honeymoons in London; visits Corsica in late winter, then travels in the region around Toulouse; leaves the Beaux-Arts after Gustave Moreau's death.

1899: Attends the Carrière studio.

1900: Works with Marquet on decorations for the Grand Palais for the Universal Exposition.

1901: Makes first submission to the Salon des Indépendents; voyages to Switzerland.

1902: Exhibits at the Berthe Weill Gallery.

1903: Exhibits at the Druet Gallery and at the Salon d'Automne.

1904: Holds first one-man show at Vollard's gallery; spends the summer in Saint-Tropez where he meets Signac and Cross; attempts painting in a neo-Impressionist style.

1905: Spends the summer in Collioure with Derain; Matisse's first fauve canvases are exhibited at the Salon d'Automne.

1906: Holds second one-man show at Druet's gallery; spends spring in Biskra and summer in Collioure.

1907: Travels in Italy.

1908: Travels in Germany; exhibits in New York, London, Stockholm, Moscow, and Berlin.

1909: Collaborates on the "Toison d'Or" in Moscow.

1910: Exhibits 66 canvases at the Bernheim-Jeune gallery; visits Munich with Marquet; vacations in Spain.

1911: Holds several foreign exhibitions; travels to Moscow.

1912: Visits Morocco.

1913: Visits Morocco a second time; holds numerous exhibitions in Europe and the United States.

1914: After being rejected for army service, he vacations in Collioure with Marquet and Juan Gris.

1915: Exhibits in New York.

1916: Exhibits in London; visits Nice.

1917: Spends summer in Touraine; settles in Nice.

1918: Exhibits at Paul Guillaume's gallery with Picasso.

1919: Exhibits 36 canvases at Bernheim-Jeune, 51 canvases at the Leicester Gallery in London.

1920: Spends summer in Etretat; designs sets for Stravinsky's *Nightingale* for a Ballets Russes production in London.

1924: Exhibits in New York, Vienna, Copenhagen, Stockholm, and Paris.

1925: Travels in Italy; receives the Legion of Honor; exhibits in London at the Tate Gallery.

1927: Wins the Carnegie Prize; exhibits in New York, Glasgow, and Paris.

1930: Spends summer in Tahiti; hold a retrospective exhibition in Berlin; travels to the United States in the fall.

1931: Returns to Nice; exhibits at the Basel Museum and at the Museum of Modern Art in New York.

1933: Works in Merion, Pennsylvania, on his wall decoration *The Dance* for the Barnes Foundation; visits Italy; creates etched illustrations for poems by Mallarmé.

1935: Creates etched illustrations for Joyce's *Ulysses* and draws tapestry cartoons.

1936: Exhibits in San Francisco and the Paul Rosenberg Gallery in Paris.
1938: Settles in the former Hotel Regina in Cimiez; designs sets and costumes for *Red and Black* with music by Shostokovich for the Ballets Russes de Monte-Carlo.
1939: Spends the summer in Paris; returns to Cimiez in the fall.
1941: Suffers from failing health; makes his first cut-paper compositions.
1943: Settles in Vence in a villa known as "Le Rêve" (the dream).
1945: Holds a retrospective at the Salon d'Automne.
1947: Is made a Commander of the Legion of Honor.
1948: Creates wall decoration for the church of Notre-Dame-de-Toute-Grace in Plateau d'Assy. Works on the design and decoration of the Dominican chapel in Vence until 1951.
1949: Exhibits in the Pierre Matisse Gallery in New York and at the Musée National d'Art Moderne in Paris; holds a retrospective in Lucerne.
1950: Exhibits at the Maison de la Pensée Française, in Paris.
1951: Exhibits in Tokyo, Germany, and several American cities.
1952: The Matisse Museum in Cateau opens.
1954: Henri Matisse dies on November 3, at Cimiez.
1956: The Musée National d'Art Modern in Paris holds a large retrospective exhibition of Matisse's works.

Photographic Credits

All works by Matisse: © Estate of Henri Matisse.
AM: Musée National d'Art Moderne de Paris.
p. 8: Exposition Universelle, © ND Viollet
p. 9: Matisse around 1900. © Archives H. Matisse—Claude Duthuit Collection
p. 10: *The Serf*, 1900–1903, bronze. Baltimore Museum of Art.
p. 12: Henri Matisse in 1896. Musee Matisse, © Le Cateau-Cambresis.
p. 13: *Orange Still Life*, AM 1972–5 (photo CH. Bahier-Ph. Migeat).
p. 14: Drawing of horse, 1900. AM 1984–80 (photo AM).
p. 15: *Studio under the Eaves*, 1903. Fitzwilliam Museum, Cambridge.
p. 17: *Luxe, Calme et Volupté*, 1904. AM 1982–96 (photo CH. Bahier-Ph. Migeat).
Interior with Goldfish, Paris, spring 1914. AM 4311 P.
p. 19: *The Green Line (Portrait of Madame Matisse)*, 1905. Statens Museum for Kunst, Copenhagen, Denmark (photo Hans Petersen).
p. 20: Nijinksy in *Scheherazade* in 1910. © Viollet Collection.
Nijinksy and Karsavina in *Le Spectre de la Rose*. © Viollet Collection.
p. 21: *The Dance*, 1910. Hermitage Museum, Leningrad (H. Matisse Archives).
p. 22: *View from the Window*, 1912. Pushkin Museum, Moscow (H. Matisse Archives).
pp.22–23: Tangiers early in the century. © Harligue-Viollet.
p. 24: French infantry during an attack in 1914. © ND-Roger Viollet.
p. 25: *Interior with Goldfish.*
p. 26: *The Piano Lesson*, 1916. Museum of Modern Art, New York (H. Matisse Archives).
p. 27: Juan Gris, *Still Life with Book*, 1913. AM.
p. 28: In Renoir's studio in Cagnes-sur-Mer in 1917. © Henri Matisse Museum, Cateau-Cambrésis.
p. 29: *Portrait of Greta Prozor*, 1916. AM 1982–426.
p. 30: Paris, the Café de la Paix in 1921. © Roger Viollet.
p. 31: The Citroën Torpedo in 1920. © Viollet Collection.
p. 32: Henri Matisse in 1928. © Matisse Museum, Cateau-Cambrésis.
p. 33: *Odalisque in Turkish Pants*, 1920–1921. AM 1071 D (photo Ph. Migeat).
p. 37: *Decorative Figure against an Ornamental Ground*, Nice, 1925–26. AM 2149.
p. 38: Lindberg in front of his plane; Lindberg in Paris. Both © Gamma.
p. 39: *Window in Tahiti*. Henri Matisse Museum, Nice-Cimiez.

p. 41: *The Dance* (first version), 1931–32. Claude Duthuit Collection (H. Matisse Archives).

p. 42: *The Back III,* 1916–17. AM 1709 S.

p. 43: *The Back IV,* 1930. AM 1711 S.

p. 44: *The Dream,* 1935. AM 1979–106.

p. 45: Pierre Bonnard, *Late Afternoon Nap.* Museum of Fine Arts, Berne.

p. 46: Panoramic view of the 1937 exposition from the Eiffel Tower. © Harlingue-Viollet.
View of the 1937 exposition with Soviet and German pavilions. © CAP-Viollet.

p. 47: *The Beautiful Tahitian Woman,* linoleum print. Pl.255, 1938. Duthuit no. 717, Bibliothèque Nationale, Paris.

p. 48: *Les Amours,* lithograph, 1948.

p. 49: Henri Matisse in 1947. © Roger-Viollet.

p. 51: *Head of Lorette, Green Background,* Paris, 1916. Matisse Museum, Nice-Cimiez.

p. 52: *The Horse, the Equerry, and the Clown,* 1943–44. (H. Matisse Archives).

p. 53: *Blue Nude II,* 1952. AM 1984–276.

p. 54: Bronze crucifix. (photo Y. Baillet).

pp.54–55: *Pale Blue Window,* design for the chapel in Vence. AM.

p. 55: Matisse working on the Chapel of the Rosary in Vence, 1950–51. © Matisse Museum, Cateau-Cambrésis (photo Dmitri Kessel).

pp.56–57: Successive states of *The Rumanian Blouse,* photos from the film by Campaux, 1945–46. Claude Duthuit Collection (H. Matisse Archives).

p. 57: *The Rumanian Blouse.* AM 3245 P.

p. 58: Matisse Museum, Cateau-Cambrésis. (photo H. Adant).

p. 59: Matisse in 1953. (photo H. Adant).